Easy to Intermediate Piano Solo

THE WORLD'S GREAT CLASSICAL MUSIC

The Symphony

60 Excerpts from 46 Symphonies by 12 Great Composers
Transcribed for Piano

EDITED BY BLAKE NEELY AND RICHARD WALTERS

Cover Painting: Jacob van Ruisdael, *Castle at Bentheim*

ISBN 0-634-03787-0

HAL•LEONARD® CORPORATION

7777 W. BLUEMOUND RD. P.O. BOX 13819 MILWAUKEE, WI 53213

Visit Hal Leonard online at
www.halleonard.com

CONTENTS

ABOUT THE COMPOSERS...

LUDWIG VAN BEETHOVEN (1770-1827).

It is difficult to know how much of our perception of Beethoven is myth and how much is fact. He was the greatest composer of his era, certainly. Beethoven began his musical studies with his father, a Bonn court musician. He was appointed as deputy court organist in Bonn when he was eleven years old. He later continued his studies with Haydn, until differences between the two ended their relationship. Beethoven was first known to the public as a brilliant, flamboyant piano virtuoso, but there was a much darker aspect to his life. He was devastated when, in his late teens, he was summoned home from Vienna to keep vigil at his mother's deathbed. The second great tragedy of his life began when he was quite young, as a slight hearing impairment. In 1802, when the composer was 32, he was informed by doctors that he would eventually lose his hearing altogether. Beethoven sank into a deep despair, during which he wrote a will of sorts to his brothers. Whether or not he was considering suicide is a subject of some speculation. Whatever the case, the "Heiligenstadt Testament," as the will is known, states that he believed he would soon be dead. He eventually came to terms with his deafness and went on to write some of his most powerful pieces. His last six symphonies were written in the following years. In addition to his nine symphonies, Beethoven wrote pieces in nearly every imaginable genre. His works include an oratorio, two ballets, an opera, incidental music for various theatrical productions, military music, cantatas, a wealth of chamber music, 32 piano sonatas, various piano pieces, some 85 songs and 170 folk-song arrangements. At Beethoven's funeral, on March 29, 1827, some 10,000 people joined in his funeral procession. One of the torch-bearers was composer Franz Schubert, who had idolized Beethoven. Some 45 years after his funeral, Beethoven's body was moved to the Vienna's Central Cemetery, where he lies near the grave of Schubert.

HECTOR BERLIOZ (1803-1869).

Credited as the inventor of the modern orchestra, Hector Berlioz was one of the most original, creative composers of his age. He used phrases of irregular lengths, striking rhythms and inventive, colorful combinations of orchestral instruments to create new sounds using the traditional orchestral instrumentation. Although hailed today as the greatest French composer of the Romantic era, Berlioz was condemned during his lifetime as eccentric or simply wrong. Even as a young man, he managed to win the Prix de Rome on his fourth attempt—only by tempering his composition to follow a traditional style that would please the judges. As a child, Berlioz studied the flute and guitar. Following his father's wishes, he entered medical school, but after two years decided to follow his own career aspirations rather than his father's plans for his future. As a result, his father cut off financial support, leaving the young composer struggling for several years. Berlioz's career was a constant struggle for acceptance. In addition to composition he worked as a music critic and as a conductor. Berlioz was tremendously influenced by literary works, particularly by Shakespeare. Among his greatest orchestral works are *Symphonie fantastique*, *Harold en Italie* and *Roméo et Juliette*. Now hailed as the greatest of his five operas, *Les Troyens* (The Trojans) was not performed in French, in its complete version, until 1969. Although *Les Troyens* is not as long as the lengthier works of Wagner, and despite the fact that Berlioz intended it to be heard in a single performance, the opera is often split over two evenings when performed. Berlioz's eventual slide into depression and illness was exacerbated by the loss of his father, his two wives and his son as well as a number of friends. He became preoccupied with death, by some accounts longing to die. His music was not to be fully understood or appreciated until the twentieth century.

JOHANNES BRAHMS (1833-1897).

Johannes Brahms was a man of strong opinions. He disapproved of the "New German School" of composers, namely Liszt and Wagner. He avoided what he believed to be the excesses of the tone poem, relying instead on traditional symphonic forms. After his Symphony No. 1 was premiered, he was hailed as "Beethoven's true heir." The symphony, written when Brahms was forty-three years old, is so clearly linked to the symphonies of Beethoven that it is jokingly been called "Beethoven's Tenth." Brahms began his musical studies as a youngster, gaining experience in composition and working as an arranger for his father's light orchestra. He revered composer Robert Schumann. On the advice of Franz Liszt he met Schumann, with whom he developed a close friendship. He also developed a deep love for Schumann's wife, Clara Wieck Schumann. From the time of Schumann's mental breakdown until his death in 1856, Brahms and Clara tended to the ailing composer. The truth of the relationship between Brahms and Clara Schumann remains something of a mystery. Brahms never married. Clara

Schumann never re-married following Robert's death. When Clara Schumann died in May of 1896, Brahms did not get to the funeral due to a missed train connection. He died the following April. Throughout his life, Brahms would sign letters "Frei aber froh" (Free but happy), until his last years when he signed "Frei aber einsam," (Free but lonely). One of the pall-bearers at Brahms' funeral was the composer Antonín Dvořák.

ANTON BRUCKNER (1824-1896).

Austrian composer and organist Anton Bruckner was one of the more controversial figures of the Romantic era. An unwitting musical revolutionary, he came of age as a composer in an era during which the concert-going public was deeply divided between the music of Brahms and the music of Wagner. He and his music were caught up in the public war between followers of the two great composers. Much of his music was not fully appreciated by international audiences until years after his death. Bruckner was a deeply religious man from humble beginnings. He was middle-aged by the time he arrived in Vienna, sporting country manners, dress and accent, and possessing virtually no social sophistication. He retained his dress and customs, and never grew comfortable in Viennese society. Part of Bruckner's social naiveté stemmed from his many years in a monastery. He was enrolled as a monastery chorister at thirteen, following his father's death, and later taught at the same monastery for ten years. He left the monastery at thirty-one, when he won the post of cathedral organist in the city of Linz. In the ten years he spent in Linz, Bruckner was exposed to the music of Wagner, which broke many of the rules of composition that he had been taught, but achieved a musical level to which he aspired. Although he became a revolutionary in his own way, he never saw himself in this light. He broke musical ground by taking Wagner's use of descriptive themes and harmonic freedom to new levels. When he was forty-four he accepted a professorship at the Vienna Conservatory, where he would spend the rest of his life. Throughout his life, Bruckner was plagued by bouts of depression, shyness and a very poor opinion of himself. The harsh criticism lobbed at him from the Brahmsians hurt him deeply.

ANTONÍN DVOŘÁK (1841-1904).

Antonín Dvořák's parents were firm believers that a child must learn to play an instrument and sing. Dvořák's father, an innkeeper by trade, was an avid amateur musician who played in the town band in Bohemia. But a career in music was unthinkable. The young Dvořák was expected to follow in his father's trade. After many battles the young musician was finally allowed to enter music school. After finishing his studies he took a job in an opera orchestra, taking on private students as well. By his mid-thirties he was supporting himself in great part with his compositions. Brahms, who later became his friend, helped him find a publisher for his work. His fame gradually spread throughout Europe and from there to the United States. In 1885 Dvořák was invited to become director of the National Conservatory of Music in New York City. In his homeland, Dvořák had been both a fan and a student of folk music. In America he delightedly found a new style of folk music to study. He was particularly taken with the African-American spiritual. Yet he was homesick while in New York. Eventually he found a small Bohemian settlement in Spillville, Iowa, where he could spend his summers speaking his native tongue and generally relaxing in familiar cultural surroundings. In Spillville he worked on his Symphony No. 9, "From the New World." It was premiered in New York in 1893 and was a huge success. In 1895 homesickness took Dvořák back to Prague, where he became director of the Prague Conservatory. He continued to compose, but the disastrous premiere of his opera *Armida* in March of 1904 hurt him deeply. Two months later he died suddenly while eating dinner.

FRANZ JOSEPH HAYDN (1732-1809).

Born into the Baroque era, Franz Joseph Haydn came of age in the Classical era. He is remembered as the "father" of the modern symphony and the string quartet. Haydn functioned as trailblazer, making the way for the likes of Beethoven, who was his student. He was born to poor circumstances, yet his family saw his obvious talent and sent him to a nearby town to live in the home of a music teacher. Although life in his teacher's home was harsh, Haydn was well taught. He went on to sing in the boy choir of St. Stephan's, where he remained until his voice broke at age seventeen. Once on his own, the young musician took a garret apartment and began working as a freelance musician, playing the violin and keyboard instruments and composing. He was eventually offered a court position, which he kept for a short time. When the Esterházy family, one of the most prominent Hungarian families, offered him a job as Vice-Kapellmeister, he immediately accepted. He remained in the employ of the Esterházy family for three decades, becoming full Kapellmeister in 1766. After the death of Nikolaus Esterházy, Haydn was granted a great deal of freedom to travel and to compose for persons other than the Esterházy family. Haydn wrote an astounding amount of music. He penned operas, chamber works, sacred music, over one hundred symphonies, as well as oratorios and even puppet operas. He was so prolific that even though his music is still frequently performed and his name is a household word in the world of classical music, the majority of his work remains unpublished and unknown.

GUSTAV MAHLER (1860-1911).

Gustav Mahler was not exactly a musician's musician. His perfectionism caused him to alienate many of the musicians with whom he worked. When he became music director of the Vienna Royal Opera he cleaned house, replacing orchestral singers and orchestral musicians. He restaged existing productions, seeing to every detail of the productions himself. The musicians considered him heavy-handed, while the opera's management felt he was spending money wildly. Mahler was a workaholic. He devoted his summers to composition since his conducting schedule during the concert season was non-stop. As a composer he devoted his energy entirely to songs, song cycles and symphonies. The symphonies are enormous, involved, Romantic works. They were brutally treated by the critics of his day. His symphonies did not find receptive audiences until after World War II, when they found unprecedented success. Mahler left the Vienna Royal Opera, sailing for New York to conduct at the Metropolitan Opera. While in New York he became instrumental in the revitalization of the New York Philharmonic. But his inability to slow down was taking its toll. Mahler had been warned that his heart was weak and was told to cut back on his working hours. Cutting back was impossible. He worked at his usual feverish pace until he collapsed in New York on February 21, 1911. Unable to return to work, he was moved to Paris for treatments. When it became apparent that he would not recover, he asked to be moved to Vienna where he died on May 18, 1911. The story has been told that in his last hours he conducted an imaginary orchestra with a single finger. It has also been said that his last word was "Mozart."

FELIX MENDELSSOHN (1809-1847).

While most of Mendelssohn's colleagues could tell stories of their battles with family over choice of career and even more tales of their financial struggles as musicians, Felix Mendelssohn could only listen. He was born into a wealthy family that supported his goals in music from the very first. Even in their conversion from Judaism to Christianity, which the family had long considered, they were spurred to action by thoughts of their son's future. It was at the time of their conversion that they changed the family surname to Mendelssohn-Bartholdy. Mendelssohn set out on his musical career with two clear goals. He wanted to re-introduce the largely forgotten music of old masters such as Bach to the public, and he dreamed of opening a first-rate conservatory. At the age of twenty he conducted a pioneering performance of Bach's *St. Matthew Passion*, the first of many such concerts he would lead. A few years later he founded and directed the Leipzig Conservatory. As a composer, Mendelssohn combined the expressive ideals of the Romantics with the traditional forms of the Classical era. He is remembered both as one of the great Romantic composers and one of the last of classicists. In his career Mendelssohn found success at an early age, and remained highly successful until his death. His sister Fanny, to whom he was exceptionally close, died suddenly on May 14, 1847. Shortly after he got the news of his sister's death, Mendelssohn fell unconscious, having burst a blood vessel in his head. Although he recovered from this incident, he was terribly diminished by the illness. His health and mental state deteriorated until his death on November 4 that same year. Memorial services for the great conductor/composer were held in most German cities, as well as in various cities in Great Britain, where he had become quite a celebrity.

WOLFGANG AMADEUS MOZART (1756-1791).

It is exceptional for nature to produce such a prodigy as Mozart. Playing capably at age three, composing at five and concertizing throughout Europe at age six, Mozart was clearly remarkable, even for a prodigy. But for nature to have placed two prodigies in one household is beyond belief. Mozart's sister Marianne (Nannerl), a few years older than Mozart, was also a prodigy and was also featured on these concert tours. The young musician's parents moved heaven and earth to further offer Mozart every opportunity to perform and study abroad. They traveled Europe incessantly. As an adult, Mozart had difficulties in his relationships with his employers, and with colleagues. Pop culture has presented us with a caricature image of the composer, thanks in great part to the film *Amadeus*, in which he is painted as a freakish, spoiled child that refused to grow up. He was, in fact, impetuous and, likely as a result of his star status as a child, often difficult to deal with. But there was more depth of personality and musicianship than the film attempted to convey. Mozart was known to complete an entire symphony in a single carriage ride, yet he chafed at accusations that it was not work for him to compose. Another factor in the exaggerated stories of his character was his inability to handle financial matters. Although he was well paid for many of his compositions, he was in constant financial difficulty. He was frequently forced to borrow money from family and friends. Mozart, who more than any other composer represents the Classical era, tried his hand at virtually every musical genre available, and succeeded across the board. In 1791 Mozart received a commission to compose a requiem. According to the terms, the source of the commission was to remain anonymous. The piece proved to be the composer's own requiem, in that he died of a 'fever" before it was completed. The circumstance of his death, and the anonymous Requiem commission, gave rise to great speculation at the time, and a film some two centuries later. In the mid twentieth century, the composer Richard Strauss is said to have laid a hand on a copy of Mozart's Clarinet Quintet and said, " I would give anything to have written this."

FRANZ SCHUBERT (1797-1828).

The story of Schubert's life reads like a heartbreaking novel. Now hailed as one of the great Romantic composers, not one of Schubert's symphonies was performed during his lifetime. It was five decades after his death before any of them were published. Schubert, the son of a school headmaster, was not a virtuoso musician. Although his musical abilities were readily apparent to his teachers, his inability to perform left him with little means to support himself. He taught in his father's school for a time, but was miserable in that job. Schubert studied with Salieri, who was astounded by the young composer's abilities. After writing his first symphony at age fifteen, Schubert presented Salieri with a completed, fully orchestrated opera two years later. Schubert lived less than thirty-two years, yet he composed a phenomenal amount of music, including some six hundred songs. One hundred and forty-four of those songs date from the year 1815, a year in which he was teaching at his father's school. After Schubert left his father's school, he had the good fortune to collect a small group of devoted friends and supporters. The friends would periodically organize evenings of the composer's music, which came to be known as "Schubertiades." Schubert's health began to fail as early as 1822. When he died, at age thirty-one, he was viewed as a composer of songs. It was not the enormous number of songs that earned him this mistaken designation so much as the fact that almost none of his other music had been performed during his lifetime. In addition to the songs, Schubert completed seven symphonies, and left one unfinished. He wrote a number of operas, although these are far from his best works. He also wrote choral works, chamber music and piano pieces. In accordance with his dying wish, he was buried beside Beethoven, whom he had idolized and at whose funeral he served as a torch-bearer.

ROBERT SCHUMANN (1810-1856).

Robert Schumann's dream was to become a pianist. As the son of a German bookseller and writer, he grew up surrounded by literature and instilled with a love of music. His world crumbled however, when he was just sixteen, with the death of his father and the subsequent suicide of his sister. Schumann entered law school, but spent most of his time studying music. In 1830 he moved into the household of his piano teacher, Friedrich Wieck. Soon afterwards, his left hand began to trouble him. His career dreams were shattered when his left hand became permanently crippled. He turned his energies to composition, making a name as a music critic as well. An inspired critic, he founded the music journal *Neue Zeitschrift für Musik* in 1834 and often wrote under the pseudonyms "Florestan" and "Eusebius." Schumann fell in love with with his teacher's daughter, Clara Wieck, a highly acclaimed concert pianist. Clara's father fought vigorously against the romance. Schumann married Clara in 1840, but only after he had taken his case to the courts. In the year he was married, the composer wrote some 150 songs, turning to orchestral music the following year. Schumann suffered from bouts of terrible depression, which became progressively worse with time. In 1854 he attempted suicide. Unable to function any longer, he was then placed in an asylum, where he spent the last two years of his life. His wife and his friend, the young composer Johannes Brahms, looked after him in those final years.

PYOTR IL'YICH TCHAIKOVSKY (1840-1893).

It is a curious twist of fate that the composer of so bombastic a work as the *1812 Overture* should have been an extremely fragile individual. Exceptionally sensitive from childhood, Tchaikovsky eventually deteriorated into a precarious emotional state. Tchaikovsky's musical abilities were already quite evident by age five, as was his hypersensitivity. His mother died when he was fourteen, a painful event that some say prompted him to compose. Over the years he was plagued by sexual scandals and episodes we might call "nervous breakdowns" today. Historians have uncovered evidence that his death, which was officially listed as having been caused by cholera, was actually a suicide. Many believe that the composer knowingly drank water tainted with cholera. Tchaikovsky's work stands as some of the most essentially Russian music in the classical repertoire, yet he was not a part of the Russian nationalistic school. In fact he was treated quite cruelly by critics of his day. "Tchaikovsky's Piano Concerto No. 1, like the first pancake, is a flop," wrote a St. Petersburg critic in 1875. A Boston critic claimed that his Symphony No. 6 ("Pathétique") "...threads all the foul ditches and sewers of human despair; it is as unclean as music can well be." For all the vehement criticism the composer received during his lifetime, his works are now among the best loved of the classical repertoire. His ballet *The Nutcracker* is an international holiday classic, while *Swan Lake* is a staple in the repertoire of ballet companies throughout the world. His *1812 Overture* is among the most recognizable of all classical pieces. In 1893 the composer completed work on his Symphony No. 6. The first movement dealt with themes of passion, the second with romance, the third with disillusionment and the finale with death. The piece was premiered on October 28. Nine days later the composer was dead.

Symphony No. 1 in C Major

First Movement Excerpt

Ludwig van Beethoven
1770-1827
Op. 21
originally for orchestra

Adagio molto

Allegro con brio

Symphony No. 1 in C Major

Third Movement Excerpt, "Minuet"

Ludwig van Beethoven
1770-1827
Op. 21
originally for orchestra

Allegro molto e vivace

Symphony No. 6 in F Major

"Pastoral"

First Movement Excerpt, ("Awakening of cheerful feelings on arrival in the country")

Ludwig van Beethoven
1770-1827
Op. 68
originally for orchestra

Symphony No. 6 in F Major

"Pastoral"
Third Movement Excerpt, ("Merry gathering of the countryfolk")

Ludwig van Beethoven
1770-1827
Op. 68
originally for orchestra

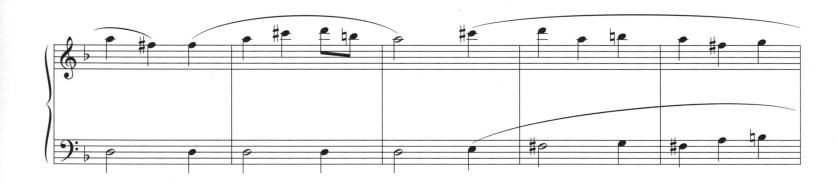

Symphony No. 6 in F Major

"Pastoral"

Fifth Movement Excerpt, ("Shepherd's song. Happy and grateful feelings after the storm")

Ludwig van Beethoven
1770-1827
Op. 68
originally for orchestra

Symphony No. 2 in D Major

First Movement Excerpt

Ludwig van Beethoven
1770-1827
Op. 36
originally for orchestra

Allegro con brio

Symphony No. 2 in D Major

Third Movement Excerpt, "Scherzo"

Ludwig van Beethoven
1770-1827
Op. 36
originally for orchestra

original key: D Major

38

Symphony No. 3
"Eroica"
First Movement Excerpt

Ludwig van Beethoven
1770-1827
Op. 55
originally for orchestra

Allegro con brio

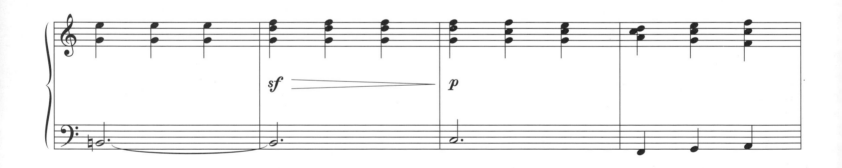

original key: E-flat Major

Symphony No. 4 in B-flat Major
First Movement Excerpt

Ludwig van Beethoven
1770-1827
Op. 60
originally for orchestra

original key: B-flat Major

Symphony No. 5 in C Minor
First Movement Excerpt

Ludwig van Beethoven
1770–1827
Op. 67
originally for orchestra

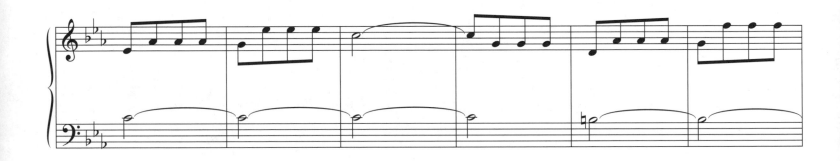

Symphony No. 5 in C Minor
Second Movement Excerpt

Ludwig van Beethoven
1770-1827
Op. 67
originally for orchestra

original key: A-flat Major

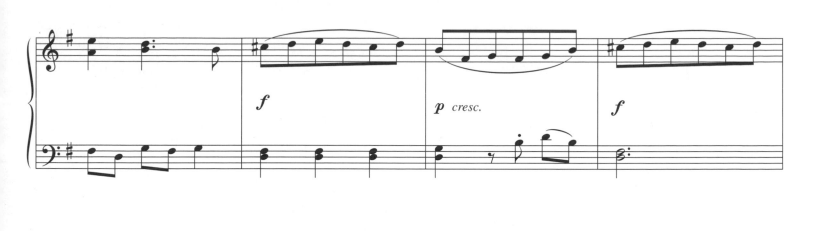

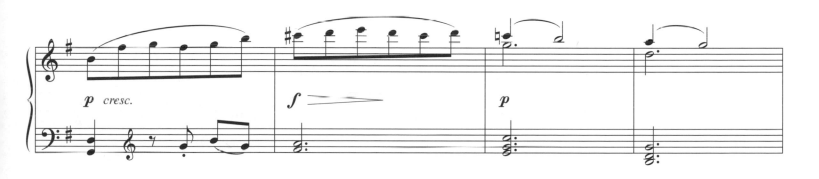

Symphony No. 5 in C Minor

Third Movement Excerpt

Ludwig van Beethoven
1770-1827
Op. 67
originally for orchestra

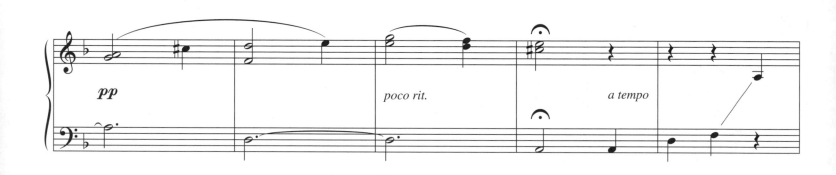

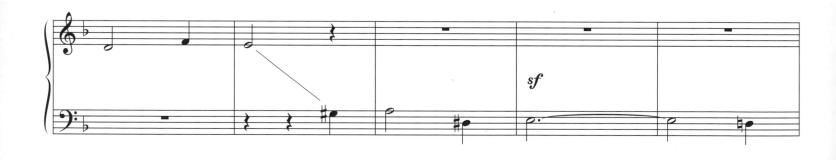

original key: C minor

Symphony No. 5 in C Minor
Fourth Movement Excerpt

Ludwig van Beethoven
1770-1827
Op. 67
originally for orchestra

Symphony No. 7

First Movement Excerpt

Ludwig van Beethoven
1770-1827
Op. 92
originally for orchestra

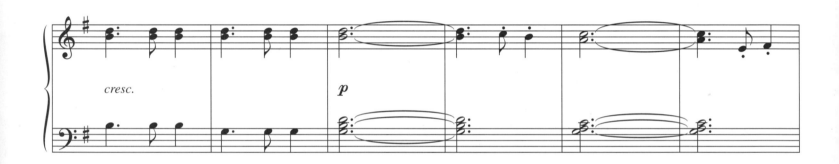

original key: A Major

Symphony No. 7 in A Major
Second Movement Excerpt

Ludwig van Beethoven
1770-1827
Op. 92
originally for orchestra

Allegretto

Symphony No. 9
Fourth Movement Excerpt

Ludwig van Beethoven
1770-1827
Op. 125
originally for chorus and orchestra

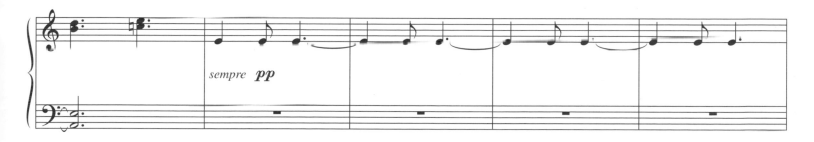

original key: D Major

Symphony No. 8 in F Major
First Movement Excerpt

Ludwig van Beethoven
1770-1827
Op. 93
originally for orchestra

Allegro vivace e con brio

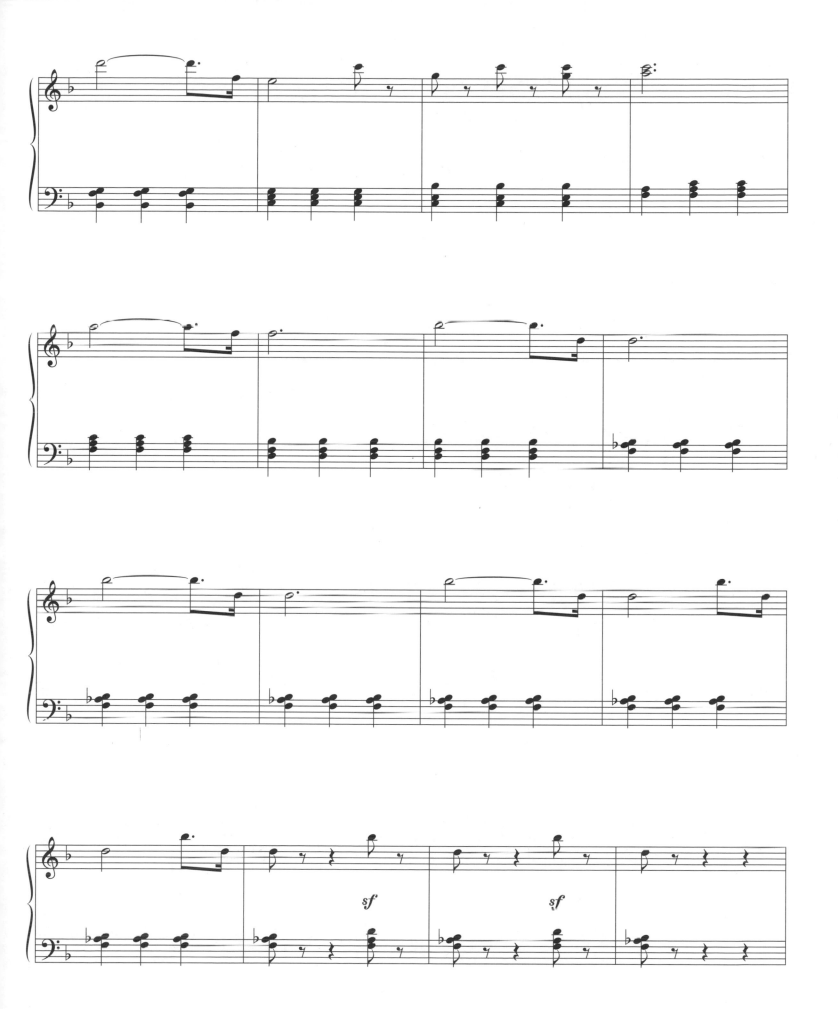

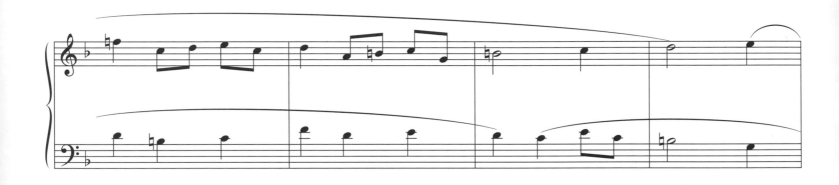

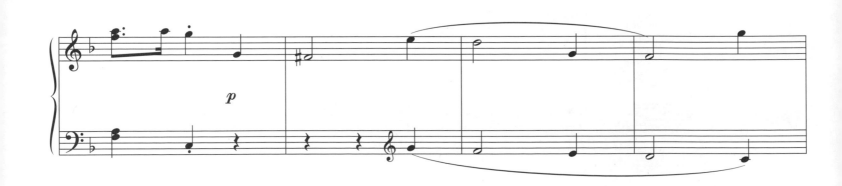

Symphony No. 8 in F Major

Third Movement Excerpt, "Minuet"

Ludwig van Beethoven
1770-1827
Op. 93
originally for orchestra

March to the Scaffold

from SYMPHONIE FANTASTIQUE
Fourth Movement Excerpt

Hector Berlioz
1803-1869
Op. 14
originally for orchestra

Witches' Sabbath

from SYMPHONIE FANTASTIQUE
Fifth Movement Excerpt, "Dies irae" Theme

Hector Berlioz
1803-1869
Op. 14
originally for orchestra

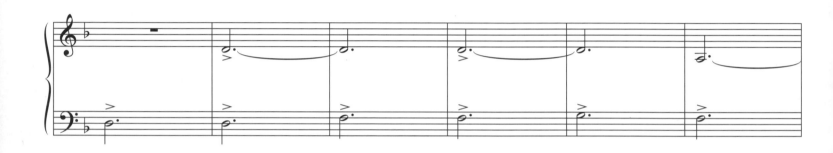

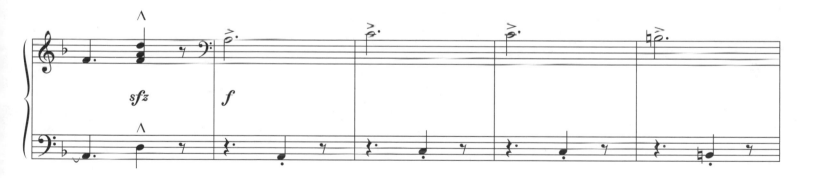

Symphony No. 1
Fourth Movement Excerpt

Johannes Brahms
1830–1897
Op. 68
originally for orchestra

Allegro non troppo ma con brio

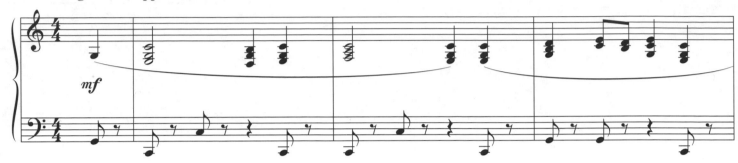

Symphony No. 2
First Movement Excerpt

Johannes Brahms
1830-1897
Op. 73
originally for orchestra

Allegro non troppo

original key: D Major

Symphony No. 3
Third Movement Excerpt

Johannes Brahms
1830-1897
Op. 90
originally for orchestra

original key: C Minor

Symphony No. 4
First Movement Excerpt

Johannes Brahms
1830-1897
Op. 98
originally for orchestra

Symphony No. 2

"Resurrection"
Fifth Movement Choral Theme

Gustav Mahler
1860–1911
originally for soloists,
chorus and orchestra

Langsam; misterioso.

ppp

original key: G-flat Major

Symphony No. 7
Second Movement Excerpt

Anton Bruckner
1824-1896
originally for orchestra

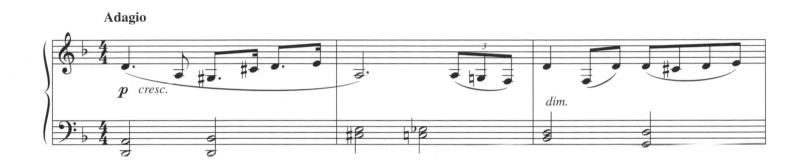

original key: C-sharp minor

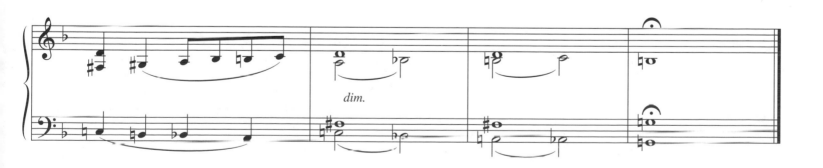

Symphony No. 4
"Romantic"
First Movement Excerpt

Anton Bruckner
1824-1896
originally for orchestra

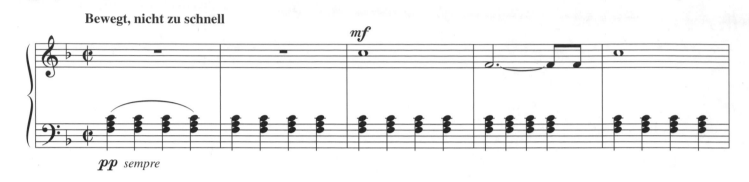

original key: E-flat Major

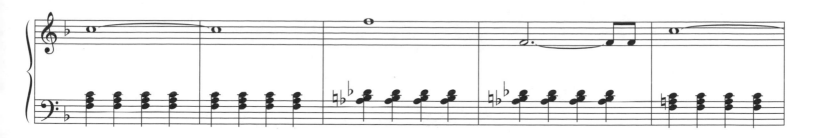

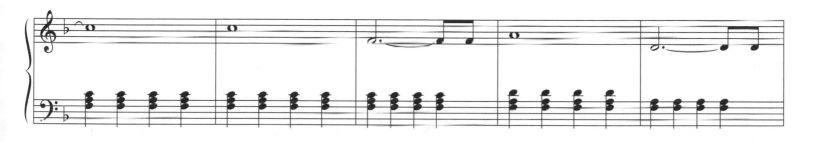

Symphony No. 8
Third Movement Excerpt

Antonín Dvořák
1841-1904
Op. 88
originally for orchestra

original key: G minor

Symphony No. 9

"From the New World"
Fourth Movement Excerpt

Antonín Dvořák
1841-1904
Op. 95
originally for orchestra

Allegro con fuoco

Symphony No. 9
"From the New World"
Second Movement Excerpt

Antonín Dvořák
1841-1904
Op. 95
originally for orchestra

Symphony No. 94

"Surprise"
Second Movement Excerpt

Franz Joseph Haydn
1732-1809
originally for orchestra

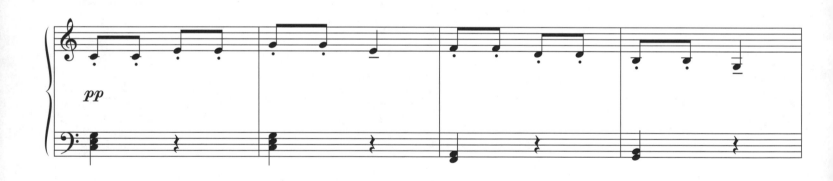

Symphony No. 101

"The Clock"
Third Movement Excerpt

Franz Joseph Haydn
1732-1809
originally for orchestra

original key: D Major

Symphony No. 104
"London"
First Movement Excerpt

Franz Joseph Haydn
1732-1809
originally for orchestra

original key: D Major

Symphony No. 1

"Titan"
Third Movement Opening Theme

Gustav Mahler
1860-1911
originally for orchestra

Solemn and steady, without dragging

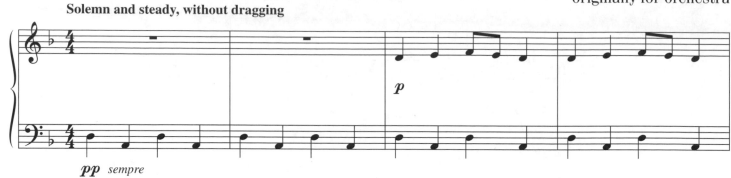

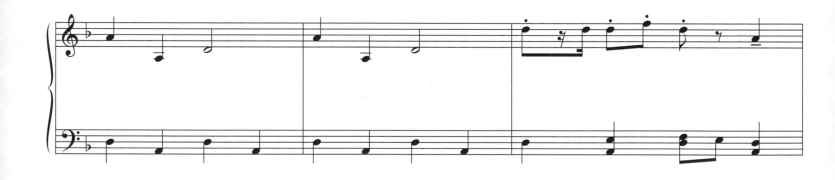

Symphony No. 4

"Ode to Heavenly Joy"
Third Movement Excerpt

Gustav Mahler
1860-1911
originally for soprano and orchestra

Poco adagio

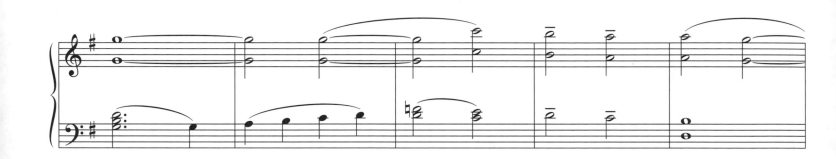

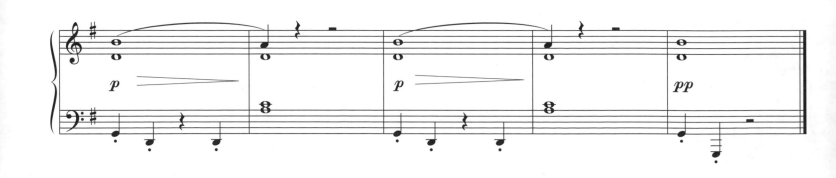

Symphony No. 8
"Symphony of a Thousand"
Second Movement Excerpt, Orchestral Introduction to the Final Scene from FAUST

Gustav Mahler
1860-1911
originally for chorus, organ and orchestra

original key: E-flat minor

Symphony No. 5
Fourth Movement Excerpt ("Adagietto")

Gustav Mahler
1860-1911
this movement originally
for strings and harp

Symphony No. 3
"Scottish"
First Movement Themes

Felix Mendelssohn
1809-1847
Op. 56
originally for orchestra

Andante con moto

Allegro un poco agitato

Symphony No. 4

"Italian"
First Movement Excerpt

Felix Mendelssohn
1809-1847
Op. 90
originally for orchestra

Allegro vivace

original key: A Major

Symphony No. 25
First Movement Excerpt

Wolfgang Amadeus Mozart
1756–1791
K 183
originally for orchestra

Allegro con brio

original key: G Minor

Symphony No. 38
"Prague"
First Movement Excerpt

Wolfgang Amadeus Mozart
1756-1791
K 504
originally for orchestra

Adagio

original key: D Major

Symphony No. 29

First Movement Excerpt

Wolfgang Amadeus Mozart
1756-1791
K 201
originally for orchestra

Allegro moderato

original key: A Major

Symphony No. 35
"Haffner"
First Movement Excerpt

Wolfgang Amadeus Mozart
1756-1791
K 385
originally for orchestra

Allegro con spirito

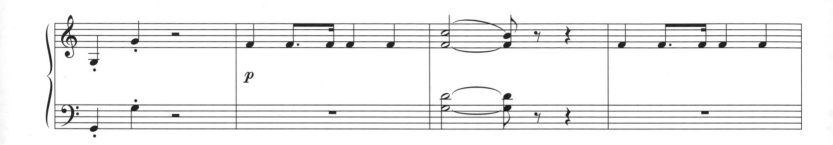

original key: D Major

Symphony No. 36
"Linz"
First Movement Excerpt

Wolfgang Amadeus Mozart
1756–1791
K 425
originally for orchestra

Symphony No. 39
First Movement Excerpt

Wolfgang Amadeus Mozart
1756-1791
K 543
originally for orchestra

original key: E-flat Major

Symphony No. 40
First Movement Excerpt

Wolfgang Amadeus Mozart
1756-1791
K 550
originally for orchestra

original key: G Minor

Symphony No. 40
Third Movement, "Minuet"

Wolfgang Amadeus Mozart
1756–1791
K 550
originally for orchestra

L'istesso tempo

Symphony No. 41

"Jupiter"
First Movement Excerpt

Wolfgang Amadeus Mozart
1756-1791
K 551
originally for orchestra

Allegro vivace

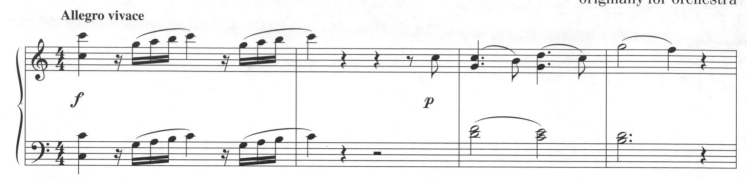

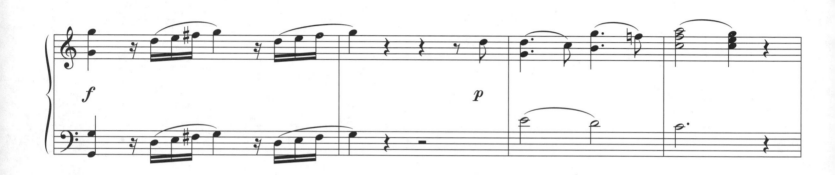

Symphony No. 41

"Jupiter"
Third Movement Excerpt, "Minuet"

Wolfgang Amadeus Mozart
1756–1791
K 551
originally for orchestra

Symphony No. 4

"Tragic"
Second Movement Excerpt

Franz Schubert
1797-1828
D. 417
originally for orchestra

original key: A-flat Major

Symphony No. 5
First Movement Excerpt

Franz Schubert
1797-1828
D 485
originally for orchestra

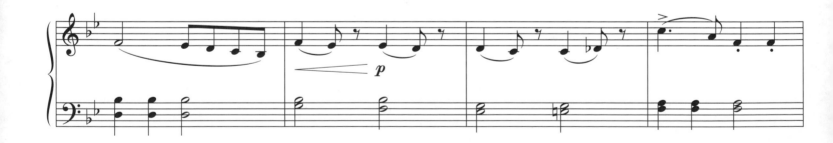

Symphony No. 8

"Unfinished"
First Movement Excerpt

Franz Schubert
1797-1828
D. 759
originally for orchestra

original key: B Minor

Symphony No. 9
"The Great"
First Movement Excerpt

Franz Schubert
1797-1828
D. 944
published posthumously
originally for orchestra

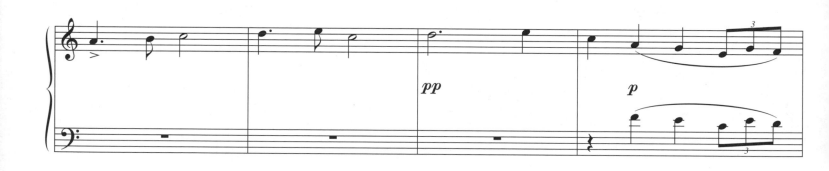

Symphony No. 3

"Rhenish"
First Movement Excerpt

Robert Schumann
1810-1856
Op. 97
originally for orchestra

Lebhaft (♩. = 66)

original key: E-flat Major

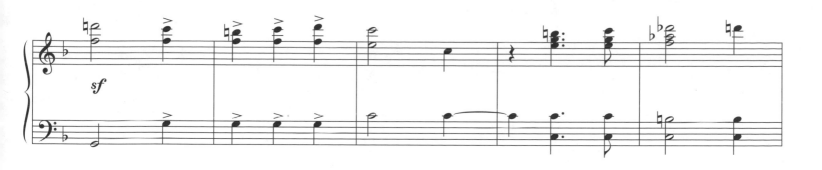

Symphony No. 1
"Spring"
Third Movement Excerpt ("Scherzo")

Robert Schumann
1810-1856
Op. 38
originally for orchestra

Molto vivace

Symphony No. 5 in E Minor
Third Movement Excerpt ("Waltz")

Pyotr Il'yich Tchaikovsky
1840-1893
Op. 64
originally for orchestra

Allegro moderato

p dolce con grazia

original key: A Major

Symphony No. 3 in D Minor

"Polish"

First Movement Excerpt

Pyotr Il'yich Tchaikovsky
1840-1893
Op. 29
originally for orchestra

Moderato assai (Tempo di marcia funebre)

Symphony No. 3 in D Minor

"Polish"
Third Movement Excerpt

Pyotr Il'yich Tchaikovsky
1840-1893
Op. 29
originally for orchestra

Andante elegiaco

Symphony No. 4 in F Minor
Second Movement Excerpt

Pyotr Il'yich Tchaikovsky
1840-1893
Op. 36
originally for orchestra

Andantino in modo di canzona

original key of excerpt: B-flat Minor

Symphony No. 6

"Pathétique"
First Movement Excerpt

Pyotr Il'yich Tchaikovsky
1840-1893
Op. 74
originally for orchestra

Andante *veneramente, molto cantabile con espressione*

Moderato assai

original key: B Minor

THE WORLD'S GREAT CLASSICAL MUSIC

A beautiful library of hundreds of great classical compositions, conveniently published in sizable volumes, all with long-lasting sewn-binding.

See our website at www.halleonard.com for a complete contents list for each volume!

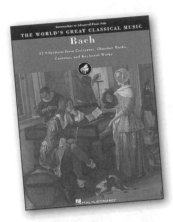

EASY TO INTERMEDIATE PIANO SOLO

BEETHOVEN
00220034......$14.95

CLASSICAL MASTERPIECES
00290520......$14.95

EASIER PIANO CLASSICS
00290519......$14.95

FAVORITE CLASSICAL THEMES
00220021......$14.95

GREAT EASIER PIANO LITERATURE
00310304......$14.95

MOZART
00220028......$14.95

OPERA'S GREATEST MELODIES
00220023......$14.95

THE ROMANTIC ERA
00240068......$14.95

JOHANN STRAUSS
00220040......$14.95

THE SYMPHONY
00220041......$14.95

TCHAIKOVSKY
00220027......$14.95

FLUTE

THE BAROQUE AND CLASSICAL FLUTE
00841550   Flute and Piano......$16.95

THE ROMANTIC FLUTE
00240210   Flute and Piano......$12.95

PIANO/VOCAL

GILBERT & SULLIVAN
00740142......$16.95

INTERMEDIATE TO ADVANCED PIANO SOLO

BACH
00220037......$14.95

BEETHOVEN
00220033......$14.95

GREAT CLASSICAL THEMES
00310300......$14.95

GREAT MASTERWORKS
00220020......$14.95

GREAT PIANO LITERATURE
00310302......$14. 95

MOZART
00220025......$14.95

OPERA AT THE PIANO
00310297......$14.95

PIANO CLASSICS
00290518......$14.95

THE ROMANTIC ERA
00240096......$14.95

JOHANN STRAUSS
00220035......$14.95

THE SYMPHONY
00220032......$14.95

TCHAIKOVSKY
00220026......$14.95

GUITAR

MASTERWORKS FOR GUITAR
00699503   Classical Guitar......$16.95

CD-ROM SHEET MUSIC

110 CLASSICAL THEMES
00220030......$14.95

FOR MORE INFORMATION, SEE YOUR LOCAL MUSIC DEALER,
OR WRITE TO:

HAL·LEONARD® CORPORATION

7777 W. BLUEMOUND RD. P.O. BOX 13819 MILWAUKEE, WI 53213